while the weeds grow

- poems to love -

JULIA C. ROBINSON

While The Weeds Grown

Copyright © 2020 Julia Robinson

All rights reserved.

All photos contained within this book and cover are by Mary Jo Hoffman https://stillblog.net/

ISBN: 9798675319695

Independently published

To Loves, past and present.

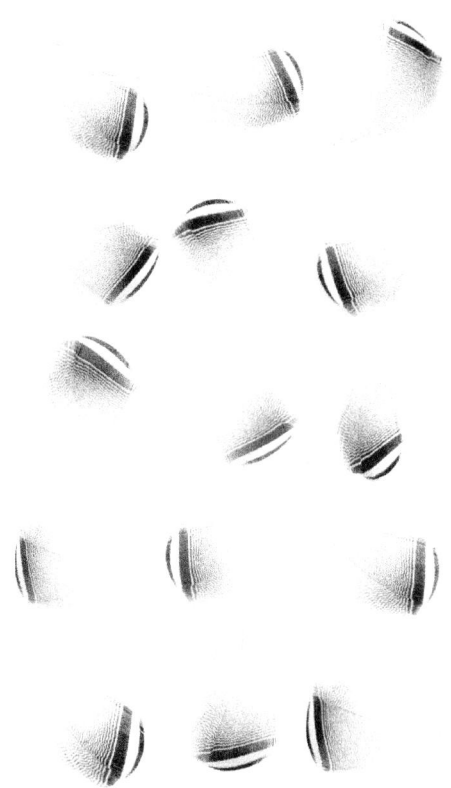

May we destroy ourselves anew.

Foreword

These poems span around fifteen years of falling in and out of love. Sorting the poems from primordial chaos into a semblance of a single relationship I began to lose sense of who and where each poem wrapped its delicate feathers around. Some poems – grounded in the fabric of the material world with mentions of caravans, trumpets and wellington boots – clearly hold the golden thread back to the precise moment of happening, but many moments of deep, life changing intimacy were left dangling out of space and time resting in the timeless fields of the heart.

As I went further, unwittingly I sculpted myself in relationship to intimacy. I saw how I love – as a human being filled with frailties and strengths, with fears and faith.

Over the years I have had experiences of being immersed in the wonder of deep intimacy, boundaries disappearing into the Oneness of being. I have also found myself flailing, trying to frantically fill in eroding gaps of painful psychic walls.

In and out, inhale and exhale, the sympathetic and parasympathetic – it is a marvel that we human beings brave coming together, coupled with the ever-present possibilities of separation.

I am humbled and grateful to those who embarked on such adventures with me. Each held the heavy mirror of my reflection, as I hopefully did for them. In moments of deep harmony, sometimes the mirrors merged and we were able finally to see.

Love. Our Self. One.

Tasting from this well imbued in me a soft velvet strength to walk into the unknown. You make the path by walking; for a path already made is not your own.

The very intention of losing ourselves to something bigger than us, of being nourished by that which we all intuitively know but cannot name, knowing that we will never be the same but will be changed irreversibly sometimes beyond recognition, is only to be treasured, nourished and admired – no matter how the story unfolds.

Ouch and ahhhhh mingle. Meanwhile the Observer, ever present, laughs with jolly mirth knowing that what is real is unchangeable, immutable, eternal.

These poems written over so many years, situations and beating hearts have helped me see how seamlessly I have been silently accompanied by Love in my delicate footing through the swamps of life.

And so, I gently realise, this book of poems is a homage to Love itself. Love, a never-ending path to where we already are.

Red

She stands,

a single poppy

– alone –

amid the rainbow

of other flowers

as if the only one -

daring to be.

Before Knowing You

I yearn to write lines of love
of you adoring something
so simple
as how I clean my teeth:
beholding me through the mirror,
my back resting on your fortress chest
my spare hand stroking
the warm forest arm
slanting up through the valley
of my well explored breasts;
a funny smile,
obstructed by the drawbridge of my
toothbrush,
becomes four
as we marvel at how
we both see
in the eyes of our reflections
flecks of life billowing brilliantly:
beautiful thoughts
bringing empty, stony echoes
into this chasm of lonely wilderness.

Beginning

Soft light

surrounds you

as I gaze

through my windows

watching

who you are.

To Be Seen

You peer in

the windows

hidden in simplicity:

a perfect hiding place.

Most walk by

too afraid to slow;

you aren't - you stop

right here

and stand

smiling too into

the sunshine.

Awakening

Droplets shine
their spectrum glory
and you are there
to see.

Hidden Love

After you have gone
and the sound of metal stairs
relax back into silence
I tingle, face abuzz,
below I am
a slippery river
over soft grateful stones.

After you have gone
I swim in the sweet silence
that nestles
after our birdsong.
Here a watershed –
a 'before you'
an 'after you'.

My mind stops travelling
in wonky straight lines

and loops happily

in merry-go-rounds

whooping, swooping,

laughing.

And also

as soon as you have gone

I fall

– sometimes gently

sometimes hurtingly –

into the memories of us

having never been together.

Effortless

Cutting vegetables

to make the pie

she realised,

wrapped in magic,

how that idea she

had yesterday

had effortlessly

materialised:

he was coming for

dinner.

Shyly

Shyly
I travel my eyes
over your slenderness
imagining your downy hairs
and slithering silk;
my tongue moves
between the gaps
of my mind,
daring to want.

Out of a Dream

I am returned

to the narrow street,

to the neighbours'

clothes hanging,

to the kiddies' bikes

chained to drainpipes,

to the cat professing

dubious love for me.

The kettle begins to boil

for night tea.

Fading fast

into a dreamt-up fantasy,

it is still real sitting with you.

Superpowers

I

She said she wanted

the super-human power

to be a fly on the wall;

but even the observer affects

their own experiment.

II

The wallflower

permeates her colour

perfuming their words

full of her unnoticed power

as the buzz of the fly

pauses the conversation.

The Second Date

The weather is confusing the flowers

who open their delicate strength

- like the fragrance of an orchid -

into the death of frost

we don't know what to think.

I burst into spring

afraid of the arrival of winter.

Kamikaze

I stumble upon my dreams
and paste them onto you
as I stroke your invisible skin.

Dangling dangerously
over the gap between
fantasy and reality
I hang on to a
kamikaze hope
of closing it.

To the Jazz Club

You brought me out

of myself

into the rain

where quite naturally

under your umbrella

you put your arm around me,

as if you always had,

and transformed me back

into a woman.

Intimate Strangers

You came with your words
full of fun and stuck them
felt-tipped on tape
on the inside of my apron –
a secret joke;
my heart is
close to there.

Our words
in the secret spot
I showed you
behind the kitchen
turned softer
more delicate
as they entered home
in heart beats
and transformed
inside of me:
new
strange
unknown.

The Simple Laughter of Sweet Joy

Under white streetlamps

and a dark navy sky

yellows, oranges, auburns

spill into the empty park.

A secret space to breathe

between us, to expand.

I kick up the leaves,

'This is what we did

when we were young...'

Childlike bliss.

'We did this...'

He bends, arms

ready for the gathering.

Hearts quicken

legs run.

I too scoop

for handfuls

the world around me

blurring in happiness.

And we play

in the middle of trees

in the middle on the night

in showers of leaves

stopping time

with the simple laughter

of sweet joy.

Bridging Worlds

You crept in

with your

wonky smile

and placed your

good ear

in a tingling hover

beside my lips

listening to

my silence.

You crept in close

and in that space

I found myself

whispering me

inside to you.

Miracle of Life

They fell

inaudibly

into silence.

Deep within

the stillness

magic stirred.

Vertigo

I fall into awe

by the expanse of a universe

rising up between our eyes

as I teeter on the edge

of your tender lips.

At the core

Down below, clear still waters.

Beyond breath.

Being.

A doorway.

Taking Heart

I feel my love

wrapped in feathers

warming in the belief

this may hatch

between us.

Providence

Seeds planted in the past

waiting in the darkness,

only a shaft of light

is needed now.

Feeling Again

Do you remember

saying last night

as the winter rain

streaked racetracks

down the pane

that you were feeling 'It' again?

That you are ready, again,

to live?

Waiting for the Evening

You fizz in me
memories of your eye lashes
butterfly through my skin.
I concentrate to get away
but you are there
ever present.
Sweet agony.
Unholy joy.

Yearning
burning, thirsting
pulls me out of
this Holy Moment,
trying to fly
into your arms
ohh so far away.

Meeting You

We have finished music making
that which simply creates forms invisible,
a dance on the sound of our souls.
After rehearsal I wait,
barely hearing the others, for you.

I see your face
stones held by winter rye
turn stars birthing in my stomach;
out of myself
I am lifted gently
a bird hurtling into the sun.

Inner silence is rarely heard
I stand by you drowning in red pride
the waterfall deafens.

Later in warm water silence

we weave threads between

the portals of our eyes.

In exploding irises

whole worlds burst open.

Love plays us

our death resurrects the now

we are taken over:

we, simple invisible forms

invisibly danced.

Do you see the movement of the dust

dancing under windowpane?

It too.

An Uncontrollable Vehicle

You turn me within.

Feeling you,

feeling me

arching my neck

into the sublime

as these swollen

lips become

an uncontrolled vehicle

towards you.

Hidden within Time

Hidden within time

the cushioned well

of Eternity.

Hotel of the Mind

I move through

my kitchen

straddling two worlds:

in one

I am slipping sugar

from a shiny spoon

into a steaming cup

of dark coffee,

in another

I am with you

there, where

only you and I

will ever know.

In Between

Words

which between

we make our own meaning.

Whirled

I am out of control

wanting;

I am out of who I was,

missing you.

Exposed.

Vulnerable.

Nakedly wandering

through a nausea

of butterflies.

Heart Moves

You walk around the corner

flowers bloom

the sun shines

and my heart

knows what to do.

Becoming

I stand naked

before you

becoming

something

more than just me.

Pillow Talk

Palatable

I taste you

deeply tender,

sticky sweet.

I swallow

not wanting

even this movement

to disturb.

We, luxuriously alive,

chokingly aware

of our essence.

Too Early?

I want to say it
but wonder
how can I?
So little
I've felt your breath.

Yet I do feel
this miracle of
soft strength.

And then
as I teeter on the edge
you say it.
You.
You do!

Blood surges
pumping.
A waterfall
flows furiously
up through me.
The throat
closes
choking words.

Into Greater Space

You say 'yes'

I say 'yes':

we gaze into

a newer us

and tremble.

Spirit Anew

Waking up alone

no more.

Fire doesn't always

burn.

Singing on a Bike Going Downhill

Only those who travel

the same speed as I,

hear the words I holler

singing out with glee.

The Ceiling Has Four Eyes Now

I got used to it
so that I liked
no one caring:
airs opened
to free glide
playing in the breezes...

The sheets hugged me
at night as I lay
star gazing
through the white ceiling
my day's dream –
known only to me.

Suddenly
You are there –
caring:
a third to enter
into the company
of me and my life.

Hidden from Winds

In the rocky sheep pen

resting on the top of the hill

we hide from the winds.

For hours upon end

we lie on our backs

secretly watching

the show of the skies;

time ours to slow.

First Sighting

I

When we went to space
we focused forces
on reaching the moon.

We're going to the stars!
We're going to other planets!
We weren't thinking of looking back.
No way!

We were ready for aliens
and the Unknown.

But once out there
we gazed back
from whence we came,
back to our planet earth

– floating fragility in infinity –

seeing ourselves quite literally

for the first time.

II

Having gone there

merging with him

I look back from Eden

and on the fall

see myself

for the first time.

The Mirror

This is me

I realise

flooded

with alarm

and relief:

this is what I have been running from.

Heaven and Earth

Taken by grace

we glide

becoming angels

flying softly through

the sensuality of matter.

Going Through Within

Past the membrane

into a secret world

we brave the soft

embrace of 'us',

forgetting ourselves

to sip for a time

of the Eternal.

Room to Grow

I am left unfinished

it is what I wanted:

to not have castle walls

cradling me in the past,

but a space to move

to breathe into

the nothingness

of these cracks within –

to peek into more

than this I am now.

Even my dreams are undone

it is what I wanted:

not to be limited

within this smallness

of being me.

Empty Mirror

Your absence

a wormhole

that sucks me

from my worlds

and rests gently

on the windowsill

as quiet as a cat

remembering,

waiting,

purring.

Burning Desire

The animal howls within

teasing me out from the spiritual

clawing for freedom,

lacerating reality.

Lips pulled back

fangs ready to attack

I am enslaved, caged

scratching at the walls.

Caress

Aloneness

catches in my throat

stings my eyes

I look up to the trees

they answer softly

with their patience.

Delight

All you did

was walk

through

the door

expected.

Counter-intuition

Falling

petrified

into the void:

a devouring mouth.

Deep within

soft kisses

brush stroke

us into nothing

but perfect peace.

Swirling Sensitivities

I feel you

inside

starling soft;

the two of us

dissolving

in a mass of

swirling sensitivities

finding their way home.

Burning Alive

I feel true.

I am alive.

Logic collapses

bewildered

by this concord

of heart and gut

wanting you.

Eventually

Eventually
the damn burst
falling slowly
soundlessly
in perfect grace:
sweet silence
after the bird song,
calm after the storm,
and the heart beating
in quiet contentment
of having worked so well.

Becoming What We Create

A new beginning.

Entering into the unknown.

All is unfamiliar

even myself.

No Going Back

How to get you out of my skin?

In my hair,

in my thoughts

in my mind.

How to get you out of my heart?

How even did you get in?

I feel sick,

nausea my new friend.

Butterflies tingle

bulldozing

through my stomach.

How to get you back

to where you once belonged?

Springs Eternal

Ohh tree

you have been here

for so long

without running

or turning away

from the rain, the storms,

the lightning strikes of life:

you simple stay here

and quietly grow

into the heights.

Here I Am

I forget
as I squirm
in my own prison
of made-up fears,
but the tree
in my heartbeat
still reaches
for the skies.

While the Weeds Grow

You cannot argue

with a lighthouse,

nor dance

with a statue.

You cannot

rely on iron

not to rust

or the rain

in England

to stay away.

You cannot

know your future

or even who will be there,

you cannot guard

from death

or disease

or heartbreak.

There is no security
that money can buy
nor poverty that
will not alter
your perspective;
there is no friendship
that will not change
your heart.

There is no child
that did not grow,
nor person who lived
without harming another,
nor an eternal
clean bill of health.

There is no garden
that will not grow weeds
nor skin that will not wither
there is no cup of tea
that will not go cold.

There is no piece of cloth

that will not wear away

and shoes do not last forever.

So what will you do?

Keep still

holding your breath,

inanely preserving

an unused life?

Or live yourself

into raggedness,

breaking, hurting, crumbling

until there is space

to see through the cracks?

Meanwhile the weeds

continue to grow.

Divine Simplicity

Growth requires risk.

What risk then

if we already know?

Acceptance

You hold me

and accept me

standing firm

smiling

amongst the volcanoes

of expression

so much so that

even I

– against the odds –

begin to accept myself.

Being a Sunday Afternoon

Warm covers

mid-winter day,

luxurious stillness.

A warm arm

wraps up

through my chest.

A warm leg

spooned.

Breath on my nape.

A soft word

quivers

in joy.

Inner Sounds

Feeling you there

holding me

I hear

chains of patterns

clatter to the floor.

Swaddled in your love

I slip out

into someone new.

Música Major

In out in out

day night day night

heart beats

boom boom

inhale exhale…

rhythm.

Music of the spheres.

Worlds Within Worlds

Looking to the stars

I feel myself

sliding once again

through the sheets of life

to where you are within.

Hidden Worlds

Between us Time morphs

into the immortal within us

I laugh and cry with you

dove tailing into our world

vibrant, alive, alight,

perfectly hidden from Cronos.

Into the Heart

This love

knits around us

stitching and pearling

our hearts into that

silent space within

soft as wool.

A Crack into Deeper Velvet

Full of soft femininity

as petals unfurl

to dewy mists,

in brave fragility

he lays open

his vulnerability.

Holding together

we stare mesmerised

into a greater sense.

Wild Root

Our souls

having breathed

in the Universal

have their own music

that swirls inside

singing out of us

in the way

only we

– each ourselves –

can sound.

Soul Sings New Overtones

Learning how to love you.
I find I am more
than I was.

Becoming Nothing

I watch time's

weather patterns

cross your face.

Our fronts meet

blowing kisses

into the dance of

the everchanging.

Nothing remains

the same.

Winds chisel

crafting this 'us'

between ourselves

as we become

slowly closer to

what we are.

Until stillness.

Until bliss.

Until 'we' break

the bonds of separation

and become not –

but All.

That Which Connects Us All

The tree listens

accepts what is

without need

nor expectations.

it softly asks us

to drop our desires

and enter into

unfolding infinities

as it luxuriates

in the bliss

of simply being.

Accepting the Here Now

It is life.

Life itself –

it is wonder enough.

Perspective

The sun never

forgives

my late rising

The waves

crash in

against my desires

Ohh Life

how can I presume

to be in control?

To Be Alone

My darling

I feel so whole

walking through

pale green leaves and autumn skies

protected by branches from the rain.

Impish joy comes from my dryness.

I savour softness within

as my feet sink into the mud of the earth.

I get close and whisper to the trees

hugging them I sense

my own presence

and how I love.

Alone, I greet myself

less a stranger now

surprised at the delicacy,

surprised how far I've come,

laughing sweetly

at the simplicity of it all.

Spirals Within

As we go around

stirring our lives

the spoon goes deeper.

Letting Go

I sit on this bench

immersed in

the heart's spectrum

and understand

that I will never, actually

understand a single thing.

Soul Mate Chemistry

Magnetised

Love between them

wrenched out all

that is not Love –

Joyful agony.

Growing into the Light

She reeled in pain

grasping onto

attachments

she no longer needed.

No Boundaries

Needing to set limits
she tumbled
like a chocolate fondue
and said the sweet thing.

Love

Down a layer

of being

into the undiscovered

tangles of being.

The pain of undoing

shears through me.

I grip on

unable yet.

Dear Ego,

Why do you stomp

up the mountain

deaf to the symphony

of fluttering flowers?

Why do you stomp

through the day

seeing challenges

as blood curdling battles?

Remember Love.

Warmly,

Your Self.

The Torment

Stop this madness!

For it is only us

- you and me –

no one else,

nothing else is happening:

look at the tree

it is gently swaying

in the storm

knowing what it is.

Anchorless

I yearn for your

solidity

of presence

that runs through

your body

to mine

anchoring me

so I may fly

to the skies for you.

Crumbling

How could I have been so blind?
You innocent,
big eyed,
vulnerable.
Me angry,
building walls
frantically
blocking you out.
In the clearing vision
tables turn
and I see
not now,
but the past,
the unworked pain
that I paste
over all I do.
And seeing it
it begins to crumble.
And seeing it,
I begin to see you
and feel ever grateful.

Lighthouse

Slowed to a silent dream
I move through the world
in a bubble of deafening
heart beats.

Suddenly I am at your door.
Legs holding.

I am ready for your fire
for your wrath.

I hold cool,
clear water.
I hold my promise
I made for you.

The door opens.
You too.

In the quiet clearing

after the storm,

love delicately flows.

Barriers collapse.

Sweet silence

softly holds us

in gentle smiles.

The Absolute Middle

In between words

meaning.

In between sky

and earth

breath uniting.

Soft Silence

Clear airs

after the tempest.

I drink in this

sweet, deep

togetherness.

You, my mirror.

You the one

accepting me

– even in my

unacceptable –

allowing me

to do the same.

Good Enough

And I realise

I do not have to be more.

The Cathedral Within

I fall into the
big silence
of the trees
as it softly opens me
into the cathedral within,
into the beauty
of seeing myself
growing invisibly
into the world.

Nothing But This

Sunlight dancing
way above
I swim deep below
where logic
happily
begins to
breaks down.

As a single unit
I lose myself –
steam-like I merge
back from a droplet
into all that is.

Sometimes
caught unaware
I scream,
but what I like the most
is to sink into it
remembering
not being
anything but this.

Sensing Death

Sharp.
Alert.
Movements
hyper defined.
In and out
bare,
raw.
No future,
no past,
no ego shouting
greedy demands.
I am nothing
but this now,
sensing the
infinitesimal,
feeling nothing
but an intense
brilliance
of simply
being alive.

The Night Before Your Flight

I lie besides you

soft snores serenade

the hours and minutes

we have together.

I break from our embrace.

Bodies one become two.

Snatched from Eden

my tree of knowledge

demands to know

the time we have left.

I am numb from wanting

this to be forever.

The Beginning of a New Journey

On the end of that pier
tears dripping into the port
my world blew up
around me
and left me alone,
totally alone,
ready to begin my path
back towards myself;
me, the intimate stranger
slowly becoming my friend.

The Golden Land

As much as you search

through this world

you will never find

what you are looking for

…for it exists not

outside.

If Only for a Moment

Between pillows

of fluffy clouds

a pink promise

of a hidden sun.

I lean my head.

Birds column dance

spiralling the winds

and for a precious moment

are absolutely still

as if desiring to feel

– if only for a moment –

their missing lover.

Faith in the Dance

It takes faith

to forget

what to do.

A leaf flutters

its dance of the wind,

a broken piece of glass

reflects the sun,

dust glorifies

the spirals of air

on the windowsill.

It takes courage to

praise the invisible

that moves us all.

Lucky

I can't but help

fall in love:

the way you come to me

with those big eyes

and pleadddddddd…

you put your head so gently

so gingerly

in my lap

and wallow in

pure joy.

It is infectious.

Who could not smile

watching that tail go?

Becoming

You may have fifteen words

for an orange

but if you have never tasted one

you have not tasted one.

Have you tasted the word 'Love'?

Jubilation

She comes to me in roses and thorns,
gliding on the wet grass,
just her wellingtons
cartwheeling her across the universe.

Remembering

I come to you

through the navy

of the night

lights shining through

light grey clouds.

Worlds collide.

I come to you

and find you surrounded

by a lush

silence of green

and remember;

and know now

why I came.

Falling into Deeperness

I like being with you.

In your depth,

I feel soft space under me

and can sink

a little more

into myself.

Lost in Time

Their bodies

an easy jigsaw:

shoulders and necks

of intertwined swans.

Each in their own centres

leaning into the other

sat on a duvet of dreams.

Post Awe

'How do you feel?'

he asks

gazing into her eyes

brushing her bare hip.

She smiles a rainbow

perfectly unable

in this glorious magic

to utter a single word.

Accepting Happiness

The tide turned:

instead of

drowning in fear

I opened out

into what

I always knew

to be true

but was too

afraid to believe.

Filled with Light

As the dotted stars

slowly shine down

from what would be,

without time,

a sky filled with light

we find the place within

that is timeless.

The Pleasure of the Valley

Allowing what is

to take us over

to become us

I fall deep within.

In the valley

in the stillness of the lake

in the beauty of being here,

me in me looking out to you in you

I see you smiling back out

into this flight path

between our eyes.

Muscles relax, open

into soft sheens of

sensuous pleasure.

Slow, ohh so slow,

we pulsate

vibrantly alive

lying in the lee

of a wind singing rock

deep within our bodies.

Realms within realms,

worlds open before me

amazed at these secret gardens.

The stillness of being here with you

rises me,

pushes me once again:

I am a kite taking to the skies.

Eternal Return

Deep breath

take mine away

so I am nothing but

a river running back

into the light

of home.

Cosmic Joke

Connecting in heavenly highs,

destroying ourselves anew

our souls intertwine

in invisible realms

before being softly,

cruelly, sent back down

to earth.

Human again.

Morning Airs

The morning airs

billow fresh through

our damp valleys.

Through my pores

I feel the smell of us

the night's heat in my cells

I feel the imprint of your lips

on my limbs so relaxed

that I wonder I can walk.

Out of Infinite Possibilities

Don't you think
it is amazing
that there is a whole entire world
full of everything you can imagine
and more than you can't

waterfalls, cages for gas cylinders in late night petrol stations, raves with hundreds and thousands of hands moving in the light spectrumed air, sun shining through dense tropical leaves seen by no human, murky brown rivers, cake shops with old ladies who don't take off their hats, early morning bakery workers covered in a fine white powder, casinos full of one-armed bandit addicts, school buses full of young worlds opening, thousands of couples right now saying 'I do' in churches and mosques and temples and beaches, hospital wards with people racked with sobs holding onto still warm dead hands, girlfriends daring a new recipe off the internet, the scream of babies

coming into the world, difficult decisions
between two almost identical products,
millions of phones bleeping right now all
across the globe,

and you and me here
right here, breathing into the same space
with no-one else around
no-one;

you

me

and these thin tin walls
flickering out of
candle shadows

you

me

in this caravan cradled
in a forgotten field
listening to the current
chorusing down a riverbed.

Just
you and me

while the rest of the world
moves on;

you and me
and the soft silence
that furs the air
broken by a crinkle of the
gluten-free chocolate cake
its wrapping crunching
as your knife searches
for a not-so-small slither to slice
and your voice saying
'How I'd like a whisky now…'
and me saying reminiscently,
'It's because the cake is so sweet,'
and you look at me and repeat,
'How I'd like a whiskey!'

You and me
here in this laboratory of two
with only this one time
and this one place.

Don't you think it's magical?
Don't you think it's a miracle?

Inner Travel Agents Unlimited

Eventually we got the fire warm
and in the blaze
you lay back
as if the sofa were
a billowing magical divan
and turned on your ears.
I felt you do so
and it gave me courage
– cor –
it gave me heart
to carry on
and describe my scenes to you;
sweet hearted you
swimming out in your love to me
- if only I will let you.
My barbaric life guard
still on day duty
as the last flickers of the sun
sink beneath us
and yet even he,
trained to protect,
dropped his guard

and let me jump
- dive even -
into the depths of me
to resurface a few
of the diamonds
I keep down there
treasuring in the dark.
I hold them in my open palm –
will you see?

From fathoms below
'Are you still listening?'
Sometimes your eyes are closed
as if dozing
yet you nod
'Yes,' soft warms tones by the hearth
'it's fascinating,'
and I believe him
and marvel
wondering where he is taking this,
what he does when this that is mine
becomes his.

My Secrets

I enjoy being with you

so much

I forget to monitor my mind

or watch my words

and I say something that

I really - really mean.

In Harmony

He stands taller than me
as we hug caressed
by a white blanketed field
of cow parsley.
Against his warm chest
through his heartbeat
I hear the vibration of his words
'Power is also being able
to not be powerful'
The river
low now
trickles by
smoothing around stones
but last week it was so high
it took away the beach.

On Soft Wings

A dawn rises within me

pink petalled and soft;

this is where you and I meet.

Template reflections.

It is beautiful.

On soft wings

I am delivered gently

into the now.

The Eternal Return

My soul settles

nestled in the

depth of feelings

sensing you

close again.

On the Ramblas

The gates to beauty open

boundaries diffuse

lighter

in the centre of a note in its true perfectness

I laugh at the ease of it all
the slow relaxed pace of delight...

floating
pure acceptance
of myself, the world, merging.

It is all too fleeting,
before I fall back into thinking;
reflecting on the autumn leaves.

Sip

A brief taste of eternity:

worth living a

lifetime for.

Ribbons of Life

Outside my window
the chickens
peck in the grass
taking the yellow
eternal flowers
for granted;

they birth, live, die
adding to the ribbons
of chickens and buttercups
filled with thousands
of starlit skies.

Through the breeze
the cow parsley waves on
totally unperturbed:
their kind has been around forever.

Under the blue spring sky
watching the clouds
move within me
I wonder
which ribbon
I am keeping alive.

Beautiful Bewilderment

I know love

like I know

fields of yellow corn

and green wild garlic

that brushes my path.

I know love

like I know

sunsets and moonrises

and the twinkling of stars.

And I know

I know nothing

as I drink blindly

from this beautiful

bewilderment

of being with you.

Innocent Fool

A yellow flower

smiles under the sun

a foot tramples it

shouting vulgarities;

the wise continue

to see beauty

within.

Into Further Truth

A flower is a flower
it decays.

Life arises
and passes away.

Life
emotions
are what are
but are not
who we are.

We too arise
and pass away –
hourly.
Nothing remains.
Nothing is permanent;
except when the 'I' is not:
which is what we truly are.

Through the Skin

Renouncing my very being

slipping through the barrier

that removes me from my name

I surrender to all.

Unbearable Ease

'What's the secret?'

she cries, desperate

for more than

mere existence.

She prostrates herself

at her lover's feet

wanting to smell only roses

'There is nothing more'

he whispers:

bare honest nakedness.

Eternal Becoming

Human ideas

once great

become stale.

Theories, isms

lose their brilliance.

Statues strutting their power

their names now forgotten.

Nature! How do you do it?

Always, new,

always fascinating.

Wondrous.

How did you become eternal?

Sleeping in the Wilds

Sparks of light:

live them

with all your life.

Find which temple

empties you out

into the world of stars.

Out of Heaven

Beseeched by sleep
seeing beauty
but no longer being it
experience fades
thoughts take over
I return to
oblivion
into the busy river
of time.

Left or Right?

The fork in the road
left or right?
The broad road
empty but easy
or
the narrow
spiny unmarked
way that
scrapes blood?

'You make the path
by walking,'
says Machado,
'On your own,'
says Hillman,
'if you are walking upon a path
then it is not yours.'

It's not only children
who are afraid of the dark.

Stranger on the Street

White hair, feet shuffling,

soon he will need a cane.

How does he keep going

into the Unknown?

The Bare Tree

Shivering naked

in the winter breeze

not even a jacket

she is so poor.

All that remains

is the dew of

glistening pearls

reflecting her

elegant beauty.

The Poor Man

So poor,

so poor,

the only thing he had

was money.

The Wisdom of Nature

She rejoices freely

in summer

though she knows it will end

not a trace of bitter fear

or moulded attachment;

graced by

natural wisdom

she lovingly shares

in abundance all the

fruits of her labour.

Our Nature

The flower wilts

unseen

we gaze

at its delectable picture

fixed in time

...and yearn to possess it.

Right or Left

In complete control,

life in my own hands,

concentration 100%

on the fast road,

motoring ahead

determined, objective, efficient.

But I wonder looking at

that quiet smile of the woman

reading a novella on the bus

if control of life is everything.

Being Now

'Be, be who you are,
tweeted the little bird,
warbling its sweet song,
'For we are all nearly dead.'
That is what caught my attention.
'But I have imagined it so differently...'
I bemoan to the little bird,
shitting from above on high.
'But how can you humans be so naïve?'
asks my feathered friend,
'So blind to the Truth?'
'The Truth of what?'
'Of happening, of arising, of passing away?
Humankind can bear so little...'
I imagine a life, an age, a year, a season, a
month, a week, a day, a second, a billionth
of a second, 13 billionths of a second, an
exploding universe, an imploding star.
'Life is what Life is!' tweeted the little bird,
'Not what you imagine it to be,'
and then flew away.

Afraid of Change

She tried to hold onto

the love that was

emanating

between them,

squeezing it dry.

Same, Same but not the Same

Months later

passing through the labyrinth

she found,

unexpectedly

the same pattern of problem;

which this time

she had the strength

not to ignore.

Memory Lane
- or -
How to Convert your Home into a Pigsty

'I'm throwing it away,' I say
with the hard edge of meaning it.
He quivers, as if I had hit him full swing,
eyes plead what his logical brain
refuses to stand for.
'We'll never use it...' I reply
into the well of his eyes,
voice softening
into his sensitivity
'...ever.'
His head falls,
as if ashamed of allowing this
to happen,
not to him
but to all it stood for.
Well aware that
Memories trap us in messy places.

The Sound of Stories Cracking

Slowly paying more attention

afraid of what I will see,

inadvertently I knock myself

off my pedestal.

Seasons

I walk alone

deepening shadows

stretch between us

under winter-tired trees

daffodils hang their sorry heads

snowbells no longer

peal wedding bells

I cannot stop them leaving.

Everywhere

I walk dreamily,

dizzily,

looking at the fields of life,

time pulls me like two dogs on a lead.

I cannot stop every time

to soak in this one particular flower

I cannot stop and consume every beauty

of every spark that dances

illuminating the others.

I must continue,

for I am being pulled by destiny.

And yet

as long as I remember

there is beauty in every field

there is nothing to regret

in being moved on.

Addicted to the Mind

We walk through the meadows

flowers burst into symphonies

the birds chorus from the skies;

you want to talk

to get away from all this.

How is it so?

Water changes

I see that

- white crests

to deep sea blue –

as I do too.

I cannot

grasp onto it,

less myself.

Between Us

My pillow

cradles the view,

a towering ash tree

pulls me through the pane.

A shadow

on the sloping field

reminds me

between us

there is a river.

Change

Curious for it to come

panic it may,

a new light beckons

at the end of the tunnel.

I cling to the dark old walls,

petrified

in wondrous awe.

Infirm-ing - Closing Within

In the candlelight

I feel the hairs on his neck

tickling my nostrils.

I don't want this bliss to end.

I hold on

grasping the moment

forcing it eternal

immobile

wanting it to never end,

never change,

dry dogma of not now.

I panic as he moves away.

Dogma

This is not the past.

I see patterns

but in predicting

I close down

this now

into what was,

shutting

the infinite

possibilities

back into the

keep of the

sterile known.

Escape

Future and past

we like them

because

we don't have to

be there.

The Light Thieves

Fears fall into me
thieves in the night
blinding me with torches:
a lightshow reflecting
of the river of despair.

Advice from a Friend

Around the marble table
- farmer's wine
not yet brewed,
the black and white floor
not quite ready -
we sip pre-season.
I whisper secrets to you,
my wise beautiful friend,
and you unwind me
out of my knots
tickling me out of
mental pigeon holes
'Forget that crap!' you say
'Live!!!
Follow your heart!'
And with your magic
you open the gate
for my return
to that place
I've never been.

To the Soprano Gitamba Oosthout

She sings

lulling me out from

cobbled thoughts

away from the streets

into the large

empty concert hall

of my insides,

a rollercoaster of vertigo

swooping through space.

Notes make a rainbow

through the limits of my body

I am carried on airs

to further within

forgetting once again where

or who I am.

Into the Light

In my mind's eye,

I see her performance

of perfect pitches.

Invisible worlds

of exquisite form,

secretly showing us

we are looking only

at shadows on the wall.

Música Major

I stare at this song
as if it were the answer
to all hidden things
as the sounds curve pathways
around the stones of my heart
and touch, without permission,
the softness of my soul.

Nothing for Nature to Overcome

The news said, 'Severe Weather Warning'.
I expected high wind and
gales through my hair
not the swirling delicacy of soft,
sensuous snow.
'It is a matter of accumulation,'
he said over text.

As the sun sets
I watch long strips of white carpet
take the form of the back terrace.
The flakes float onto the slats of wood
or fall through the gaps to the forest floor.
Long parallel universes,
growing white high
an inch or so.

The gentle army
– trillions of
one-off crystals –
fall
and
fall
and
fall.

Some stick to the side of the slat valleys
capriciously catching on
as if gravity did not scare them.
Others follow suit
till the sides of the parallel universes
unite the individuality of the rows
into one single plane.

Over the hours mesmerised by the
white changing landscape
I wonder, if things, if history, if our lives
are as predictable as weather patterns?
That if we have enough opportunities
pitter-pattering through our lives
will we eventually form
the unimaginable, obviously?

Perhaps everything happening to us
always would have:
that our tiny little drop
is part of a whole
unimaginable to our senses
and the seemingly
unbridgeable gaps and breakages
in what we call our lives
are nothing at the end of the day
for nature to gently overcome.

Birds of Migration

We meet again

in our Spring

fluffing our feathers

and chirping news

sitting by the sea road

coffees between us.

I fly in his gaze

somersault in his words

wondrous at the joy of

connecting again

after our long, long winter.

Light of You

Find the eternal

Here Now

for there is nothing

outside of time.

Clear Heart

A clean glass
transmits light.

Tap Root of Trust

I don't know how we came
to be such mirrors.
Where do you end
and I begin?
It hurts this drifting apart.

And then suddenly
from deep within
the land of whispers
a door opens between us
sending scents
of love and laughter
and a deep tap root of trust.

And, like a branch
that goes on growing
despite the fragile fibres
of a clumsy break,
we each find it
in our hearts to feel
– within the settling wilds –
our love again.

The Return of the Sun

Your soft words

drizzle over me

as I unfurl

into this

shaft of light.

Returning to You

Returning to you

as no-one

I find you are

more than

I thought you were.

Dissolving

In the night

I come to you,

empty mind

blank space,

open.

You pour into me

into the space

we make,

dissolving ourselves anew.

Rejuvenation

In my silence

his silken hands

stroke

my landscape,

fingers gently

ploughing

bringing air

back into my soil.

Delight of You

You lean on the big dark

moss dribbling wall

laughing

at something funny

sparks flying in your eyes

sharing something naughty.

Just good friends,

as well.

Unknown Ad Infinitum

Tomorrow

breathes

butterfly kisses

on the neck of my now;

but isn't yet.

Will it?

The Joys and Horrors of Being in Love

I go down into love

snorkel, mask and tanks

prepared for the pressure.

We swim together

sharing secrets untold.

Another world

flows between us

as tangible threads

weave currents connecting us

under the white sheets of dreams.

Increments of Awareness

Drip drip drip

the rock is slowly

transformed.

Hurts like hell

this sting of being human,

of being sculpted

and not the sculptor;

ever more naked

to the simple

unfolding of Life.

Becoming Real

I dream

I am being held

and wake up

within your arms,

feeling your chest

as my own.

This is not a dream.

This is not poem.

This is.

Open

I

I stand simply

small in the vastness

of the valley

listening

to the wind in the trees

as wind in the trees.

Heart silenced

it hears so much more.

II

I breathe in this Now;

no need to heal

that which is

already healed.

Ease of Being

I notice the ease that

a half-filled cup of tea

exists so easily on the table,

how the tree outside

has never complained

through snow, rain

and shine

and how I too

am actually here

simply, peacefully

doing the same.

Dance and Dancer

We dance in the space to love

as the confines form our steps.

For how can we be without them?

Billowing Behind

I let go

trusting these arms

this embrace.

Feet move

by themselves;

I, myself, float

– leaving my

gliding body

in its echoes

of pleasure –

to soar

through the music

into a world

– secret from eyes, ears

and this contact of skin –

to be nourished

by the soft silence

billowing behind.

The song ends,

I return startled

as the room forgotten

bursts into view.

?

Is the other a limit?

Or do they set you free

to open into The Nothing

and become

all you ever were?

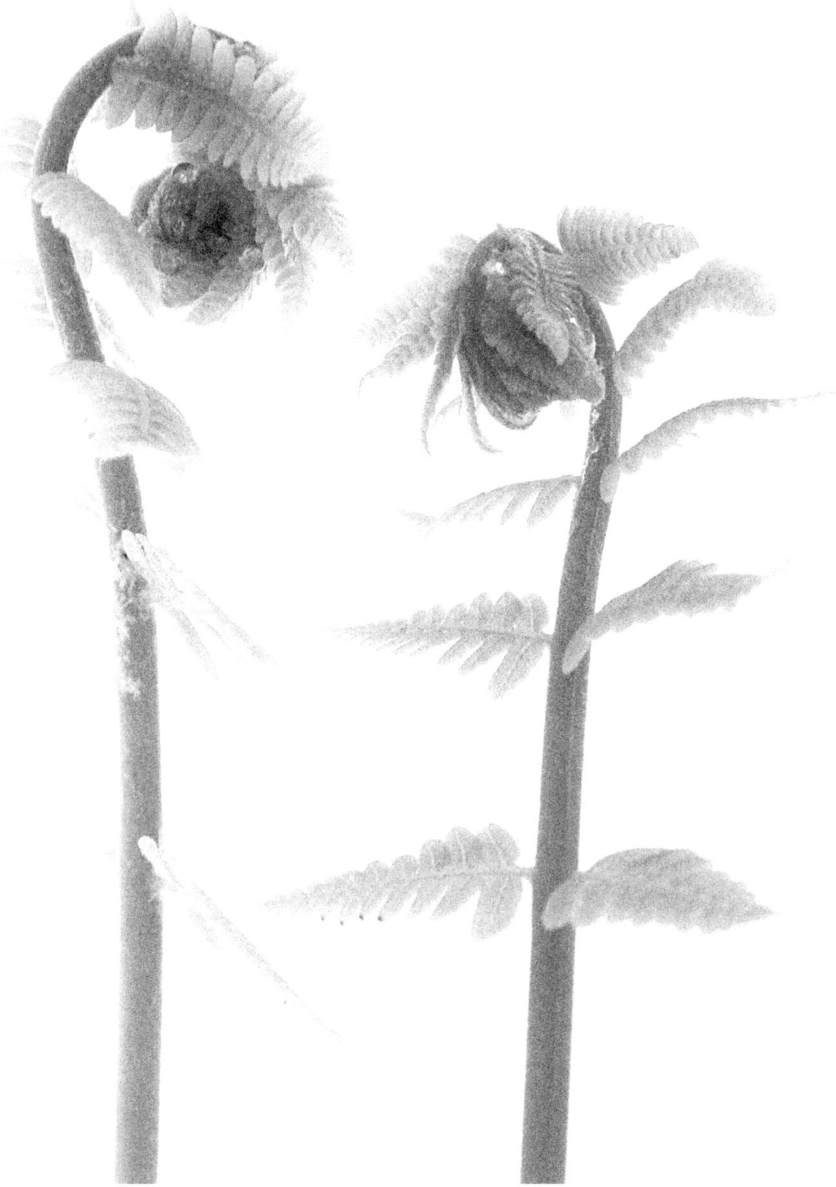

Julia Robinson has spent her life out of the box, hitchhiking around the world, floating down the Amazon in a self-made raft, selling roasted chickens in Argentina, working at an orphanage in Nepal, studying a masters in Jungian psychology in Spain, going to art school in Greece, dancing and writing in the States and is presently playing the trumpet and writing in Latvia – she has a curious mind, an adventurous spirit and a thirst for the unknown.

For more prose, poetry and graphic explorations into life please visit:

www.intenselypersonal.com

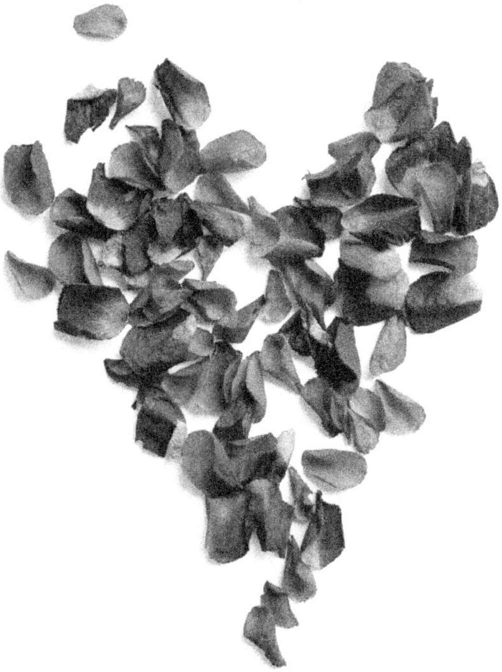

INDEX

Red	7
Before Knowing You	8
Beginning	9
To Be Seen	10
Awakening	11
Hidden Love	12
Effortless	14
Shyly	15
Out of a Dream	16
Superpowers	17
The Second Date	18
Kamikaze	19
To the Jazz Club	20
Intimate Strangers	21
The Simple Laughter of Sweet Joy	22
Bridging Worlds	24
Miracle of Life	25
Vertigo	26
At the core	27
Taking Heart	28
Providence	29
Feeling Again	30
Waiting for the Evening	31
Meeting You	32
An Uncontrollable Vehicle	34
Hidden within Time	3

Hotel of the Mind	36
In Between	37
Whirled	38
Heart Moves	39
Becoming	40
Pillow Talk	41
Too Early?	42
Into Greater Space	43
Spirit Anew	44
Singing on a Bike Going Downhill	45
The Ceiling Has Four Eyes Now	46
Hidden from Winds	47
First Sighting	48
The Mirror	50
Heaven and Earth	51
Going Through Within	52
Room to Grow	53
Empty Mirror	54
Burning Desire	55
Caress	56
Delight	57
Counter-intuition	58
Swirling Sensitivities	59
Burning Alive	60
Eventually	61
Becoming What We Create	62
No Going Back	63
Springs Eternal	64

Here I Am	65
While the Weeds Grow	66
Divine Simplicity	69
Acceptance	70
Being a Sunday Afternoon	71
Inner Sounds	72
Música Major	73
Worlds Within Worlds	74
Hidden Worlds	75
Into the Heart	76
A Crack into Deeper Velvet	77
Wild Root	78
Soul Sings New Overtones	79
Becoming Nothing	80
That Which Connects Us All	82
Accepting the Here Now	83
Perspective	84
To Be Alone	85
Spirals Within	86
Letting Go	87
Soul Mate Chemistry	88
Growing into the Light	89
No Boundaries	90
Love	91
Dear Ego,	92
The Torment	93
Anchorless	94
Crumbling	95

Lighthouse	96
The Absolute Middle	98
Soft Silence	99
Good Enough	100
The Cathedral Within	101
Nothing But This	102
Sensing Death	103
The Night Before Your Flight	104
The Beginning of a New Journey	105
The Golden Land	106
If Only for a Moment	107
Faith in the Dance	108
Lucky	109
Becoming	110
Jubilation	111
Remembering	112
Falling into Deeperness	113
Lost in Time	114
Post Awe	115
Accepting Happiness	116
Filled with Light	117
The Pleasure of the Valley	118
Eternal Return	120
Cosmic Joke	121
Morning Airs	122
Out of Infinite Possibilities	123
Inner Travel Agents Unlimited	126
My Secrets	128

In Harmony	129
On Soft Wings	130
The Eternal Return	131
On the Ramblas	132
Sip	133
Ribbons of Life	134
Beautiful Bewilderment	136
Innocent Fool	137
Into Further Truth	138
Through the Skin	139
Unbearable Ease	140
Eternal Becoming	141
Sleeping in the Wilds	142
Out of Heaven	143
Left or Right?	144
Stranger on the Street	145
The Bare Tree	146
The Poor Man	147
The Wisdom of Nature	148
Our Nature	149
Right or Left	150
Being Now	151
Afraid of Change	152
Same, Same but not the Same	153
Memory Lane – or –How to Convert your Home into a Pigsty	154
The Sound of Stories Cracking	155
Seasons	156

Everywhere	157
Addicted to the Mind	158
How is it so?	159
Between Us	160
Change	161
Infirm-ing - Closing Within	162
Dogma	163
Escape	164
The Light Thieves	165
Advice from a Friend	166
To the Soprano Gitamba Oosthout	167
Into the Light	168
Música Major	169
Nothing for Nature to Overcome	170
Birds of Migration	172
Light of You	173
Clear Heart	174
Tap Root of Trust	175
The Return of the Sun	176
Returning to You	177
Dissolving	178
Rejuvenation	179
Delight of You	180
Unknown Ad Infinitum	181
The Joys and Horrors of Being in Love	182
Increments of Awareness	183
Becoming Real	184

Open	185
Ease of Being	186
Dance and Dancer	187
Billowing Behind	188
?	190
About Julia Robinson	193

More books by Julia Robinson

Bedtime Stories for Adults

Prose

Poetry　　　　　　Poetry　　　　　　Poetry

For more information please visit
www.intenselypersonal.com

Printed in Great Britain
by Amazon